God's Best Is Your Child

A Home School Mom's Teacher's Guide in Etiquette & Character for Children & Teens

*In Correlation with **God's Best Is Me**; Living To Please God*

by

Dr. Jeanne Sheffield

http://www.SouthernGracePlaceUSA.com

or

http://www.JeanneSheffield.com

authorHOUSE®

AuthorHouse™
1663 Liberty Drive
Bloomington, IN 47403
www.authorhouse.com
Phone: 1-800-839-8640

Published by AuthorHouse 5/9/2013

ISBN: 978-1-4817-3368-7 (sc)
ISBN: 978-1-4817-3367-0 (e)

About the Author

Dr. Jeanne Sheffield's life has transitioned as a professional performer in show business in variety television in Los Angeles, to her exciting always challenging position as founder and director of Southern Grace Place USA located in Washington, DC.

Today Dr. Jeanne wears many hats as inspirational singer, composer, voice, piano, character, and etiquette teacher, and author. She holds a Masters degree in Christian Counseling and Doctorate in Theology from Jacksonville, Theological Seminary in Jacksonville, Florida

Dr. Jeanne Sheffield's mission is for parents, their children, and teenagers of America and around the world to learn and appreciate the value of *God's Best Is Me* studies. Her program, and this companion teacher's guide, was created to cover many issues facing our youth today.

Congratulations, Mom!

You are about to start an exciting and rewarding six weeks ahead as you teach kids Christian etiquette and character based on the noble attributes of Christ. No one else is better suited for the job than *you*. And do you want to know the best part? You have the advantage of knowing what study habits your children have, their strong and weak points, and how to introduce them to new life concepts that they haven't fully embraced until now.

For these next six weeks, you'll encourage your children to imitate the impeccable etiquette and character of Christ in all they do. You'll see how God will bring out the *very best* in your children as you teach manners, communication, social skills, and godly principals. What a privilege it is that God has entrusted you to pour so much of His character and refinement into your children! Think how delightful it is going to be to see these young sprouts grow to become a shining reflection of Jesus.

Preparing for Class Time

Before we begin with the initial training, there are four 'must have' teaching aids and one bonus that I should mention to you.

I. Mom's Lesson Guide

Includes Weekly Lessons, "**Mom's Tips**" and a Creative Ideas section to make your classes interesting and exciting each week.

II. Mom's Idea Notebook

Purchase a spiral bound notebook for jotting down new ideas, prayers, and journaling about your children's progress. Also have extra pencils and paper handy for each child.

III. Student Workbook

A six week workbook entitled "God's Best Is Me." This "fun-to-learn" topical study educates your students about the character and leadership of Christ which includes valuable social skills and etiquette.

IV. "God's Best Is Me" Praise Songs CD

An original collection of inspiring and up lifting praise songs highlight certain topics for kids and teens to sing each week. Examples are praise songs about the importance of a good attitude, over flowing joy, giving our love and walking in grace. See our web site http://www.SouthernGracePlaceUSA.com to order.

V. Home Business Guide Bonus *"The Home School Mom's Marketing Ideas Packet"* provides ideas on how to turn this 6 week study into a home business so you can teach other children for profit.

How To Make This Course
Fun & Rewarding

This *Teacher's Guide Book* is designed to make it easy to follow along with each week's study. It will give you fun ideas that will cause your kids to participate and interact with one another. You will enjoy teaching your kids not only educational studies, but it will help you to easily follow along with each week's study and assignments.

To avoid being stressed over what to cover in each chapter, *you have the option of choosing which topics you want to teach each week*. This book offers suggestions for you to consider topics that work well with each other, so that the information will be comprehensible. It is up to you to decide what topics work for you within your time frame. Whether this is your first time at teaching or whether you are a seasoned home school leader, you will find the **Moms Tips** included throughout this book to be helpful in each chapter.

Table of Contents

Song Book Table of Contents

The *God's Best Is Me* Song Book & CD accompaniment can be ordered by:
Telephone: 202-716-6444
Email: DrJeanne@SouthernGracePlaceUSA.com
On-Line: http://www.SouthernGracePlaceUSA.com

Week One
Love

"The mediocre teacher tells, the good teacher explains,
the superior teacher demonstrates and
the great teacher inspires."
-William Ward

Begin The Day With Prayer: You and your children may want to hold hands in a circle as you begin a prayer. Invite the Holy Spirit into your studies to guide and direct you as you teach. You may want to ask for prayer requests. Praying together is always powerful and brings closeness and care for each other.

This Apostle's Pledge:
> ** See Creative Ideas Create Attention/ This Apostle's*
> *Pledge to create ideas for an Apostle's Pledge poster.*

"I pledge allegiance to you, Lord Jesus, that I will walk in your grace and peace. Create in me Your Temple, Lord, where You will want to be. Make my life your vessel. Fill me with your Living Word, so I can go and share Your Love with those who haven't heard."

Mom's Tip: As a mom and teacher, you want your children to be strong leaders. Show the children your poster (place on an easel) of 'This Apostle's Pledge' and explain why they will want to be like Apostle Paul, who followed faithfully in the foot steps of Jesus and became a great Christian leader. Have them cross their hearts and recite this pledge promising to follow it's instructions to share the love of Jesus with every one. This should be memorized and is to be recited every week.

Acts of Grace:

Please, Thank You, Excuse Me, You're Welcome.

These four actions in grace are meant to instill awareness and appreciation of others. Their purposes are to be in tune with our surroundings and to be considerate and thoughtful. Make sure your students practice **The Acts of Grace** each week and require them to memorize them. Every week ask them to tell the class *how, when and where* they practiced their personal Acts of Grace:

* How did it make them feel?

* Did the Acts of Grace help to make a positive difference for someone?

* What does it mean to go the extra mile?

*See Creative Ideas Create Attention/
Acts of Grace poster ideas

The Fruit For The Week: *Love.* There are nine Fruits of The Spirit and you will want each student to memorize them all, however, we will focus on the first six to compliment this six week study.

Sing Songs of Praise:

One the highlights of this study is singing and expressing praise songs about God's love. Your students will look forward each week to this segment of their studies as they learn new songs and have lots of fun singing together.

* Introduce, Listen and Practice the "God Brings Out The Very Best In Me" CD.

* Play the CD two times while the students read the lyrics to the songs and sing along with the CD to become familiar with "The Fruit Of The Spirit" song and "God's Best Is Me".

Mom's Tip: Choose which praise songs you want your students to learn. IF time allows, be sure and repeat the same praise song that you practiced the week before and add a new one each week. You may find that they always ask to sing "The Fruit of The Spirit Song" each week

It's very important to allot a specific time period for your praise songs, so you won't get behind time for the rest of your lesson plan.

Don't be overwhelmed with the following topics in your first chapter. They all flow together and move along quickly. If you feel you can not get all the topics in each week's time frame, then save them for the next week or include them with another week's study.

Some students command a lot of attention and like to tell the class stories. Do not let them *monopolize* your time. Be in charge of your class and pace yourself by paying attention to the time you have allotted for each topic. Time each topic allowing a few moments for class participation.

So that you will feel confident while teaching, practice ahead of time speaking aloud and time each topic allowing a few moments for class participation.

Chapter One Topics:

- My Appearance
- The Mirror My Friend
- "Cool Manners" Make "Big Impressions"
- Saying Hello and Goodbye
- Your Handshake
- Conversational Skills
- Introductions
- How To be A Good Friend
- What Qualities Should You Look For In A Friend?
- Character Traits of Friendship

Fruit For Memory: Matthew 27:37-39. *"Love the Lord with all your heart and with all your soul and with all your mind. This is the first and greatest command. And the second is like it. Love you neighbor as yourself."* Each fruit has a special scripture which you will want your students to *memorize* and *recite* the following week.

Mom's Tip: **Challenge your Students.** For a fun incentive, challenge your students to learn all six week passages and give them a *special reward* at the end of the study. It is important to have your students bring their Bibles each week, which can also give them another challenge to look up other scriptures.

Mom's Tip: **Stimulate Change and Variety.** To keep interest, kids like change and variety and you will want to keep their interest at all times. If you have more than one room or an adjoining room, take advantage of your space. Tell them, "Ok, it's time to recite Your Apostle Pledge and The Acts of Grace. Let's all move to the side room", for example. Never stay in one place for too long. Even taking them outside on the patio or underneath a tree for a topic study would be fun and interesting. Children love variety.

The First Topic:
Appearance

Begin with the students taking a close up and personal look at their own appearance. The image they present to the world is very important. Have fun discussing the message they will want to portray to others and why.

Materials: Mirror(s) Use a mirror to pass around the table or have a small mirror for each student.

My Appearance
Why Should I Be Modest?

Children and teens should learn that it only takes two minutes or less to make an initial and favorable impression with someone. Turn to page 15 and read the first three paragraphs to the students. This is the time to start their first open discussion about their personal appearance.

Talk about the issues of being feminine and masculine. Have them follow along in their work books as you facilitate and create an inquisitive atmosphere. Get them thinking and excited to participate, but keep the study flowing. You have lots of fun and interesting topics to cover this first week and you'll need to make the most of your time. Ask them what do they think about the way boys and girls dress today as you all read the student's work book together.

The Second Topic:
The Mirror, My Friend

The mirror shows us a true reflection of what we express to others. It is the face we will want the world to see. This first exercise begins with the children observing their own facial expressions. Using a hand held mirror ask them to make a big smile and then a big frown. Watch their reaction. Ask, "What's the difference between a smile and a frown?" Talk to them about facial expressions and how they can affect others positively and negatively. Ask if they like the face they see. Ask them what kind of expressions do they think they use most of the time. You're bound to hear a few some surprising observations and some cute giggles! Have them follow along with the student's work book comments on page 17.

The Third Topic:
Cool Manners Make Big Impressions

Read how and why Eye To Eye Contact is a major factor in meeting a person. Turn to page 17 in the work book. This is a great topic to discuss. Ask each child to look at each other in their eyes and introduce their names. Talk about why speaking their name with confidence is so important. Tell them to be proud of who they are and the name they have been given. The work book comments are very useful here. It's giggle time again!

The Fourth Topic:
Saying Hello and Goodbye

It's time to discover inter-active role playing on page 18. Students now need to read their work book. Select two girl students to play the characters in Example 1. Choose which character you want each one to play.

First, let them read the scene aloud. Next have them stand and portray the scene on their feet. For more confidence, you may want them to do it again.

Mom's Tip: You will find that your students love scene studies. If you have time, choose another set of kids to do Example 1.

Choose two kids to play Example 2. Start the same way as Example 1. Read the questions in the work book and listen to what the students have to say in reply.

The Fifth Topic:
Your Handshake

This is a *must do it over again fun* topic located on page 19. Have lots of fun showing the three kinds of hand shakes and have all the students join in with different partners. Read the work book explanation of each one aloud. These are:

1. The Bone Crusher
2. The Limp Fish
3. The Firm Hand Shake

As their teacher, you are establishing the firm hand shake as a good foundation for developing excellent conversational skills and confidence. Practice the firm hand shake with different partners throughout these six week classes. For fun, tell them to practice all of them with their friends and family. It's a fun exercise for everyone!

The Sixth Topic:
Conversational Skills

The student's work book on page 19 is all you need for your reference. Pair up every child with a partner. If you have a shy child, invite him or her to join in.

Mom's Tip: If there is withdrawal or rebellion, don't pay attention to it or waste time coaxing. Generally a child will catch on and fall in. If not, give them another week to adjust.

The Seventh Topic:
Introductions

Adults rarely meet a well-mannered child these days. A child or teen that has impeccable manners and poise has an edge over other young people and they seem to succeed better in life. That's why you must encourage your students to pay special attention to this exercise. Practice introductions with every student and have them practice at school and with their friends. Entice them to practice these skills with their teachers and with their parents. This is how we as teachers can take a clueless kid with no manners and teach them to have refined communication skills that will make them stand out as someone special with confidence and finesse.

The Eighth Topic:
How To Be A Good Friend

Creating The Spirit of Friendship
What Qualities Should You Look For In a Friend?
Character Traits of Friendship

Mom's Tip: Friendship is a subject your students will really want to participate in. Take time to read the work book's information on pages 22-23 regarding the qualities to look for in a friend, the character traits of a friend, and how to correct a friend in love by reading this section aloud with your students. The facets of friendship are very important for young people to understand, especially during the formative years.

The exercises on pages 24-25 are examples of what to look for and not to look for when looking for a friend:

Exercise 1. The Disappointing Friend is an example of a jealous friend. Choose two role players and read through the script. Set up two chairs facing each other and hand each one a cell phone. Choose another set of students to play Debbie and Felicia. Read their work book's foot notes and ask the students these questions.

Exercise 2. Being a Good Friend is an example of a true friend. If possible, choose two more students to portray these close friends. Read the work books notes aloud. Ask the students what they think about loyalty and trust. Why is it so very important in friendship?

Mom's Tip: Choose one student to read the "Real Good Friend" poem. Prepare 8 1/2 x 11 hand-out sheets with a colorful design for them to write about their best friend and have them read it to the class next week. All the students enjoy doing this! You will probably not have time to hear all of the reports, so have two read theirs and then add two more each week. Then everyone will have their moment to share.

Be An Active Fruit

On page 29 in their work book the students will see several different suggestions for giving their love this week. Encourage them to practice each one and to give the class a report of what they experienced in the next week. Remind them of the Lord's first command, which is *"Love the Lord thy God...."* Ask them how does God want them to do this?

Work Book Weekly Lesson Review

Good for you!! You and your students have now completed all the topics in Week One. Before you end the class with prayer tell the students that they will have 'Fun Work" to complete, which are the exercises starting with Chapter One's fruit of Love on page 28. Here they will write what they learned about valuable character values and social skills each week to become a genuine demonstrator of "The Fruits Of The Spirit." Turn to this page and explain what they should do in these exercises. This is a weekly review which you will expect them to complete each week. Choose one student to give their report to you the following week.

Mom's Tip: You might consider giving each student a little treat at the end of their studies each week. Examples: *Cookies, candy, pencils about character or achievement, etc. Teacher supply stores carry a variety of treats for kids.*

Already you and your students have covered many topics in Week One. I hope you and your children had a great time!! You have given them a lot of new information, discussed ideas and opinions, practiced good communication skills and portrayed good and bad behaviors. You have sparked their interest and started the ball rolling and next week will be even more fun!

Closing Prayer

Hold hands and ask the children if they have any special prayer requests. If so, give them to the Lord and pray a prayer of protection over them during the next week. Pray for God to show them ways to love like Him and to practice the fruit of Love to everyone they meet.

Week Two
Joy

"A good teacher is like a candle. It consumes itself to light the way for others."
Unknown

Your students are back again and excited for the second week studies. There's energy in the air and they are all revved up to learn, practice and sing their new praise songs with you.

Mom's Tip: Let's review your weekly outlined format before you introduce each week's new topics and gauge your time.

Mom's Tip: Remember to always prepare your posters and any loose materials ahead of time.

Begin The Day With Prayer

This Apostle's Pledge: Read poster together

Acts Of Grace: *Please, Thank You, Excuse Me, You're Welcome*

Fruit For The Week: *Joy*

Praise Songs: Sing "God's Best Is Me". Introduce and listen to another new song from the praise and worship CD.

Mom's Tip: **Add Some Fun Staging**: Mostly all kids like to sing and perform. Some don't. Don't let withdrawals or shyness stop you. Singing positive, up lifting songs about God and life fills their spirits with joy! Put them in front of a mirror if you have one. Shy students usually warm up and join in. You are the teacher, so carry on! You don't have to be a professional choreographer. Have fun with them! Some children have great staging ideas. You want to keep their interest sparked not only in music, but throughout this study.

Materials:

An artificial apple, orange, cluster of grapes, and a banana.
CD Player
"God's Best Is Me" CD
A wide full length Mirror, if possible.

It's always good to line up your students according to height *(tallest usually on the ends and shortest in the middle)* with a mirror. If you do not have one, then consider the front porch, the driveway or the back yard. You need enough space for them to spread out their arms. This is always a fun time, so don't worry about the perfect setting.

Example 1:
Staging "The Fruit Of The Spirit" Song

Spread each student with arms length apart. Place them in one row. If you have more than six, place them in two rows. Stagger the back row so the audience can see them. Delegate each fruit to a certain student. Each time an apple is sung for example, have that student take a step forward and hold up that fruit for every one to see. When the students sing the line *"you might as well hear it* 'cause the Fruit of The Spirit is love, joy, peace, patience, kindness, goodness, faithfulness and self control," have each student turn a sharp left as they say each fruit and then turn a sharp right facing front as all the fruits are sung. The last fruit, <u>self control</u>, can be sung to each other to remind themselves to especially practice this important fruit.

At the end of the song have them shout out to the audience "Chew On The Fruits!!" *Their audience will love it at graduation, if you choose to sing it!*

Use your own creative ideas for staging, too. Encourage the students to think of some creative ideas. Just have a great time!

Example II
Staging "God's Best Is Me"

This is the theme song of the students work book and CD and it should be an important one for you to emphasize. The best approach is to have the students sing the words with a sincere heart. Use motions that are simple to compliment the song.

Example III
Staging "Love Stretches My Heart and Make Me Feel Good Inside"

Use Stretch Exercises: This is a free expression song suggesting that the students stretch and move freely. Make sure your students are able to bend and stretch enough to spread their arms out wide. Have them open their arms wide on the line "God's love stretches, God's love stretches. God's love stretches when you open your arms wide. *(make arms big and wide).*

Chapter Two Topics:

- Attitude = Gratitude
- Check Your Attitude
- Punctuality Is A Habit You Can Master
- Exercise Punctuality

Fruit For Memory: Proverbs 15:30. *"A cheerful look brings joy to the heart, and gives good health to the bones.*

"Move the students to their study table and have them open their Bibles to this scripture which is about the second fruit, **Joy.** Ask one student to read it aloud, then have all recite it.

Review Week One: Ask who did their "Fun Work" exercises on page 28. Ask what five character values did they learn last week? What five skills did they practice using the fruit of Love? Ask one or two students to give you their answers.

Mom's Tip: Make sure that your students understand how important "Fun Work" is to develop in character and communication skills. Consider a special treat to those who have finished their work each week. *(This will give those who didn't do their work an incentive to complete their assignments each week.)*

Be An Active Fruit: Talk with the students about sharing their joy for Jesus with their friends. Have them look at the examples their work book gives them to keep a positive attitude all week and the ways they can share the joy at home, school and in all their activities.

Workbook Weekly Lesson Review: Page 28 reviews the fruit of *Love*. Ask them what did Chapter One teach them?

Ask if they practiced what they learned. Have them give you examples. This week was focused specifically around friendship.

Again, they are expected to complete the five character values and five skills they learned this second week featuring friendship.

Telephone Etiquette

Children and teens are notorious for yelling, mumbling and stammering on the telephone. Some do not have the slightest idea how to take a message or write down a phone number. Sometimes they reveal personal information that no one should know. Read all the information on page 33-34 in the work book with the students. Select certain students to portray Kevin and Tom. Change their names if you have only girls.

Mom's Tip: Be sure to let your students know how important it is to close a conversation. Sometimes people's feelings might get hurt without saying goodbye. Poor telephone etiquette habits can be corrected. You now have an opportunity to correct these things or any particular problems such as these mentioned above with your students.

Go by the student's work book and use the following materials:

1. A tape or digital recorder.

2. 2 cell phones.

3. Note paper and pencil for each student.

4. Practice writing and recording each student's out-going message with a *smile* in their voice.

5. Practice a 2 way conversation between students with one taking down a message.

6. Take a vote: who spoke the clearest?

7. Who had a smile in their voice?

8. Who closed the conversation with "goodbye"?

9. Who took down phone numbers? Pass around the message notes.

10. Whose message notes had the best information and whose was the most legible?

Mom's Tip: Radio Shack, Best Buy or Target have new, relatively inexpensive small digital voice recorders with excellent clarity. You can also find them for sale on line. Use these as a tool to play back to the students how they sounded on the phone.

Attitude = Gratitude!

Nothing is more important than attitude. It can turn a gray sky blue or turn your life and even those around you up side down. A good attitude is the key to success in every situation. A positive attitude is *powerful*. It is about the most important topic to *master*, except for the Bible studies and scriptures you have to teach during this study.

Exercise 1

Emphasize the importance of a good attitude as opposed to a bad attitude. Pass the mirror around again and let every student look into it and say *"Hello You Wonderful You!"* Their work book tells them to start each day with this slogan. Ask them to practice it all week and have them tell you if it made a difference.

Exercise 2

Give them a piece of paper and tell them to write down ten people they are grateful for. Next, tell them to write ten things they are grateful for. If there isn't enough time in your lesson plan for this, you can have them do it for next week's fun work.

Exercise 3

Demonstrate to the class the appearance of slumped shoulders and a frowning face. Ask them what kind of an attitude does this person have? Demonstrate straight shoulders and a happy face. Ask what kind of attitude does this person have?

Check Your Attitude

Ask each student to check their attitude to see if it is the best it can be. Ask them to think about some things they do or say that could be corrected. Read exercise 1 and 2 together on page 35 and choose two students to portray David and Jason. Discuss Jimmy's attitude. Do you know of people who are like this? What do you think about what David and Jason said to Jimmy? Was it the right thing to do?

Mom's Tip: Create a weekly "My Attitude Check List" to review every night before going to bed. Make up a scale for them ranging from of 1 to 10 with one being the *poorest* attitude and 10 being "My Very Best Attitude." Tell them to be honest with themselves and to check each day to see what changes they have made throughout the entire six weeks. This will help them in areas where they may be weak and it will help them as they rely more and more on the Fruits of The Spirit to strengthen their attitude in all situations. By putting on their very best attitude they will be pleasing to God and everyone around them. Remind them that God is expecting them to follow His commands so that He can call them His *Very Best Examples* every day.

Have a class discussion about when they have had good and bad attitudes. How did they feel about themselves? If you have boys in your class, this is the time to let them shine in Exercise 1 and 2 in their work book. If there are no boys, the girls can still role play the characters.

Punctuality Is A Habit...Master It!

Being punctual tells a lot about who we are and how we value other people's time. You can take this moment to show your class how they can learn to be a disciplined *'on time'* person and a *'dependable'* person who shows respect for others. Read page 36 together.

Exercise In Punctuality: Students who have been in theatre particularly like the exercise on page 37. Choose two sets of students to practice this exercise in punctuality. Be sure to describe this situation and ask the questions from the student's work book.

Be An Active Fruit: This week the students have the opportunity to practice *Joy*. Show them how they can practice being a joyful person in every situation this next week on page 38 in their work book. Explain that joy comes from having a good attitude, and by practicing joy when we're happy and even sad, because God is always with us. The work book tells them many ways to practice joy through the week.

Weekly Lesson Review: Ask who finished their "Fun Work" exercises. Who read the suggestions of how to live in joy at the end of chapter two? Who felt joy in their hearts this week? How did it happen? Share with us. Have them answer five character values they learned this week and the five skills they learned about how to be a joyful person.

Closing Prayer

Week Three
Peace

"Teaching is the greatest act of optimism"
Coleen Wilcox

By now your students have become familiar with their lesson plans, their praise music, and what they are expected to do each week. Continue reviewing and introducing them to more new topics. During your lesson plans challenge them to think and to participate in all their studies, activities and exercises.

Begin The Day With Prayer

The Apostle's Pledge   *(Recite Poster*)

Acts Of Grace   *(Recite all 4 Acts)*

Fruit Of The Week: *Peace*

Praise Songs: Repeat: God Brings Out The Very Best In Me
The Fruit Of The Spirit Song
Love Stretches My Heart
Introduce:
*Are You A Real Good Friend?

Topics: True Obedience is Worth Mastering
Rude Is Crude & Polite Is Nice
Rude Is Crude Exercises
Tactfulness
Good Sportsmanship

Fruit For Memory: *"Peace I leave you; My peace I give you. I do not give as you as the world gives. Do not let your hearts be troubled and do not be afraid. John14:27*

True Obedience Is Worth Mastering

Turn to page 43 and talk with the students about what God expects of us. What does His Word say? Have them fill in the blanks in the third paragraph. Make sure they understand what "True Obedience" means and why it is important to their future in all that they will do in life. Emphasize *mastering* "True Obedience.

On page 44 you will find a True Obedience Weekly Chart List, which your students can put on their fridge or in their room to complete for next week's assignment. Have them make notes. Have them rate themselves *honestly* from one to five with one being low and five being the highest score.

Rude Is Crude & Polite Is Nice

Read aloud page 45 with the students. Have them check what they think of America's behavior today in the 21st century. Being rude is an offensive type of negative behavior. There is never any excuse for it. Spend time emphasizing how important it is to be kind, patient and considerate in all situations.

On page 46 are examples of scripture and what the Bible says about the words we use. Tell the students to pay attention to what Jesus says.

Mom's Tip: A worth while suggestion would be for them to memorize the prayer in paragraph three. It is a wonderful way to start the day or at any time we catch ourselves thinking negatively about someone. This prayer reminds us to think and speak like who?? Jesus!

Rude Is Crude Exercises

Exercise 1
On page 47 are fun exercises for the students to practice together as a group. Choose two actors to portray the scene and everyone read together. Next have everyone stand up and get in line for the movie. The actors portray the scene. Ask those who stood in line what they thought of this person's behavior to the other person that they interrupted.

Exercise 2
Read the scenario between brother and sister together and then choose two characters for Jamie and Gary. Choose another two actors so that the children all have an opportunity to portray different behaviors.

Mom's Tip: It's always good to ask questions and stimulate your student's thoughts. Use your own questions if something comes to mind that will add to this topic and to other topics to keep your studies exciting and interesting.

Tactfulness

Tact is The Way To Act

On page 48 you have a good definition of the meaning of tactfulness. You might choose one student to read this aloud. Have them think of someone who is a typical example of a tactful person. Read all the material in the first three paragraphs.

Exercise 1: All read the script. Choose someone to play Tiffany and someone to play Linda and Susan.

Read the questions and listen to the students reactions to this scene. Ask who else would like to play this scene? You can change the gender if you have boys in your class.

Exercise 2: All read the script. (See page 49.) Select someone to play Maggie and Alexis. Notice your student's reactions.

Discuss all three topics on rudeness, being polite and being tactful which you have just covered. Ask your students what did they learn about being rude and crude? Why is being polite and nice the best behavior to have? Why is being tactful right? Why should we care about other people's feelings?

What does God's Word say about how we should treat each other? We should *edify each other*. To edify means to build each other up. Building another person up makes them smile and have confidence. It makes us happy to see others.

Good Sportsmanship

Good sports always check their character within

The most important attribute of a person is their character. The way we treat others and the way we live our lives says so much about who we are and how we were taught to value others. On page 50 read the first paragraph to your students. Have them check the important character traits and discuss experiences they have had that were positive or negative. Ask if they had another chance to behave differently in a situation what would they do? Read them the last paragraph which explains how being a good sport is being a "Quality Person".

Be An Active Fruit One of the greatest challenges in life is to live in peace, especially when things are very disruptive around us. The Lord reminds us to rely on Him and not to be troubled because why? He is our *Peace*.

Weekly Lesson Review Tell the students to read page 51 and to practice the many ways to live peacefully within and with others.

Review Week Two: Ask what the students learned about taking messages on the phone? What kind of voice should they have? What information should they write down? Why is attitude important? What kinds of attitudes do we have? How can we check our attitude? Did you check your attitude every night this week to see how you rated from one to ten? How well did you do? Are you an on time person? Are you considerate to others? What are some ways we have learned to be a punctual person?

Fruit For Memory verse: John 14:7 *"Peace I leave you; My Peace, I give you. I do not give you as the world gives. Do not let your hearts be troubled and do not be afraid."*

Close in Prayer

Week Four
Patience

"Only a life lived for others is a life worth while."
Albert Einstein

Begin The Day With Prayer

The Apostle's   *(Recite the poster)*

Acts of Grace   *(Recite all four Acts)*

Fruit For The Week: *Patience*

Praise Songs: **The Fruit Of The Spirit**
                God Brings Out The Very Best In Me
                Love Stretches My Heart
                Are You A Real Good Friend?
                *Attitude Is Your Gratitude *(several optional CD choices)*

Introduce: **Attitude Is Your Gratitude Song**

Topics: What Is Etiquette?
           What Is Integrity?
           Who Is A Quality Person?
           The Meaning of a Quality Person
           Becoming A Quality person
           The Many Ways We Can Be Respectful
           Respect Exercises
           God's Dreams For You
           Dreams Do Come true

Fruit For Memory: **Psalm 37:7** *"Be still before the Lord and wait patiently for Him."*

What Is Etiquette?

Begin this week by asking the students if any one knows what the word etiquette means. (1) *Etiquette is a French word that means conventional or socially acceptable, or required in a society or profession.* An easy definition for children to learn says: *(2) Etiquette means to be "polite and considerate" in all kinds of situations.* (See page 55)

Mom's Tip: Expect your students to memorize the second definition for etiquette next week.

Ask them if they know where or how etiquette began? Explain that etiquette began in the French royal courts in the 1600's during the reign of King Louis XIV, who was planning a formal dinner. He used a *placard*, a word which means an announcement of a future event that he posted for the people to see. This was the start of formal invitations.

Ask the students if they can think of other countries who may have different etiquette than our standards of etiquette in America. Examples: *(Japan, Africa, England).* Ask what they have observed about these cultures and do they think *they are* different than ours.

Should we learn the kinds of etiquette other countries use before we visit there? Yes. It will make the people of that country think we took the time to understand their ways of doing things and we will feel that much more comfortable while visiting there. We can also discover the ways in which our culture is different from theirs or the ways in which it might be much the same.

A Good Example of Being
Polite and Considerate:

Always show people respect when they think enough of you to include inviting you to something special.

If you are invited to a special event by mail, it is always good etiquette to call and accept an invitation by telephone or if the invitation is formal, to accept by mail. *(This is called R.S.V.P. which is located at the bottom right of an invitation.)* It is always appropriate to regret not being able to attend an invitation.

Pay attention to the date of the function and always reply with your acceptance or regret respectfully within a week or ten days before the event. Not responding to an invitation is rude and it makes people lose respect for you, which may cause them not to invite you to another event.

Types of Etiquette and Good Behavior:

There are many different kinds of etiquette. Here are some examples:

Table Manners *being confident in knowing proper table manners. behavior; having a pleasant attitude; including everyone in conversation.*

Telephone Etiquette *is a polite, cheery voice to hear.*

Punctuality *means it is always important to be on time.*

Conversational Skills *are knowing how, when & what to say.*

Good Sportsmanship *means winning and losing gracefully.*

Tactfulness *is being careful to be kind and considerate.*

Always say "The Acts Of Grace"
practicing please, thank you, you're welcome and excuse me.

Introductions *means knowing the proper way to introduce and meet others (refer to week one)*

Examples of Different Kinds of Etiquette

- teacher/student etiquette
- doctor/nurse etiquette
- police/citizen etiquette
- employer/employee etiquette
- minister/church secretary

Ask the students if they can think of more examples.

Impress upon your students that by practicing good etiquette you will have a special polish and shine about you when others look at you and hear you speak. Good etiquette impresses others that you have been educated with excellent communication and social skills, because you are poised and confident being who you are in all situations. Who knows? You may one day have the privilege of accepting a formal invitation to join the President of the United States and his wife for dinner at the White House! That would be a grand opportunity for you to practice what you have learned.

Good Etiquette Makes People Notice YOU!

Discuss the many ways we show etiquette with the bullet points on page 55 in the work book. Ask if they can think of other kinds of etiquette.

What Is Integrity?

Integrity is a noun that means *completeness, wholeness, soundness, sincerity and honesty.* Have everyone read the definition of integrity aloud on page 56 and expect them to memorize it for next week's class.

(Offer a special treat for those who know it when you review.)

* Read all the questions and discuss.
* Explain that integrity as well as one's character is a person's most important possession.
* Explain that people notice your character in many ways.
* Ask them to think about how they think others notice them.
* Ask them to take a few moments and search inside their hearts to see if they are a person with integrity?
* Is there something they could improve upon?
* Do they do the right thing when no one is looking?
* Ask who do they admire the most? Why?
* Who has more integrity than anyone? Why?

Who Is A Quality Person?

Turn to page 56 and discuss the meaning of a "Quality Person." Why should you want to be one?

Discuss the character traits of a non-quality person on page 57. Ask the students to look at themselves and see if they have any negative character traits? How do they think they can correct these traits?

Discuss the questions asked on this page in their work book. Ask why should you want to be a quality person?

The Meaning of a Quality Person
Becoming A Quality Person

Read pages 57 and 58. Check the list of a non-quality person on page 57 to see if there are non-quality traits that you need to correct. Everyone read the character traits of a Quality Person on page 58. Check the ones that exemplify you. Make it a special moment to point to Jesus as being our supreme example of thoughtful etiquette, character, integrity and leadership.

The Many Different Ways
We Can Be Respectful

Have each student read an example of ways to be respectful on page 59.

Respect Exercises: Lack of respect and obedience is a major issue for many children and teens toward their parents and other people in authority.

Mom's Tip: Suggest keeping a daily "Respect Journal". Write in at the end of the day how you showed respect to your parents, siblings, teachers, friends and people who have authority over you. If you did not come up to what you know you should do, ask God to help you to improve your attitude and behaviors tomorrow. Keeping track of how your respect others will increase your own self respect.

Read Respect Exercises on page 60 for homework this week using their "Respect Journal" to show how many ways they showed respect to their parents, teachers and friends.

Home Work

Next week will be a fun time to share from their **Respect Journals**. Be sure to emphasize that they all write down their experiences in showing respect to those in authority. Ask them the following questions:

* Did someone notice that you were being respectful?
* How did you feel about yourself?
* Did anyone notice a change in your attitude for the better?
* Did anyone notice that you were more respectful?
* If so, how did they react?
* Let's discuss what keeping a "Respect Journal" has done for you and those important people around you.

God's Dreams For You

It is so important for children to realize that God thought of us even before He created the world. Ask them to stop and ponder this a few minutes. Have everyone turn to Psalm 139:13 and read what David says to the Lord about God knowing him before he was born. *It is also important for you as their parent and teacher to encourage them to dream and imagine.* Some of the greatest world inventors, artists, composers and thinkers were dreamers. Dreaming and imaging is a wonderful gift God gives us. Just imagine how God must have dreamed to create this is amazing, marvelous world in which we live. Have you ever dreamed about the beauty of heaven? God says our eyes and ears have never seen such beauty!

Read the first two paragraphs aloud to the students on page 62.

Ask each student to read an inspiring quote about dreams. Ask your students if they have special dreams for their future that they would like to share.

Examples:

- *What do they want to do when they grow up?*
- *Where do they want to go to college?*
- *Do they want to marry?*
- *Do they want children*
- *Do they want to be single?*

Dreams Do Come True: On page 62 read to them why God gives us dreams and imaginations. Help them understand the many reasons that God put dreams into our hearts when you read the first two paragraphs aloud to them.

Read together: Ask these questions about your dreams. Have the students share their *dreams.*

My Dream Poster

Children love to make posters, especially about their dreams. This gives them an opportunity to think about their future, what they would like to do, where they would like to live, or who they would want to marry, etc. Get them excited about making their poster a creative project and encourage them to design it colorful and interesting for the class to see!

- Prepare ahead with enough colorful posters for each child. Let them choose which color they want. *(find posters at drug stores, dollar stores, Michael's)*

- Collect magazines for them to choose pictures and to get ideas.

- If possible, have them create their posters on a table or a floor that won't be damaged with glue. *(another option: spread out a wide sheet of work paper on the floor for them to create.)*

Materials

- Colorful Posters
- Use Rainbow Magic Markers
- Glitter Glue
- 2 or more Scissors
- Clever Stickers *(Dollar Tree Stores, Michael's)*

(If you are running out of time, have them take their posters home and create them for the next week. Be sure to give them an option to use your stickers and to put the title of their dream and name on the poster. Examples: Rachel's Dancing Dreams or Michael Wants To Fly.)

- *Have each student stand before the class and explain the meaning of their poster and why they chose to create it.*

- Consider voting on the most interesting poster.

- Take their "Dream Posters" outside and take a class picture. Make a copy for each student to keep as a special memory.

Be An Active Fruit: Patience is a very special fruit to master, because in the world we live we so often want things instantly. Sometimes we want things selfishly. Sometimes we are impatient with ourselves. Pay careful attention to the points given you to practice this week with patience. Review page 65 every day and you will see how your patience improves with everything you do.

Weekly Lesson Review: Remind the students to read how they can show *Patience* this week on 64. Have them write character values they learned this week and five skills they can exercise to show *patience* this week. Remind them to memorize the definitions of etiquette and integrity. Ask if they understand who a quality person is and who isn't. Why? Remind them to be respectful everyone, especially to God and their parents.

Week Five
Kindness

"To learn and never be filled, is wisdom,
to teach and never be weary, is love."
Unknown

Begin The Day With Prayer

The Apostle's Pledge   *Recite by Heart*

Acts of Grace   *Recite by Heart*

Fruit of The Week: *Kindness*

Praise Songs: The Fruit of The Spirit Song
God's Best Is Me
Love Stretches My Heart
Attitude Is Your Gratitude
Are You A Real Good Friend
(*optional* Choices from the CD)

Topics: Being A Lady
Being A Gentleman
Writing Notes
Jealousy Can Eat You Up!

Fruit For Memory: Proverbs 16:14, *"Pleasant words are a honeycomb sweet to the soul and healing to the bones."*

Being A Lady

This topic found on page 69 lends itself to fun and interesting conversation with young girls. It also gives you an opportunity to explain where inner beauty begins and to stress the importance of being a lady in all situations.

Read aloud with the girls all the written material and tips for being a lady in their work book on pages 69-70.

Mom's Tip: It would be fun for you to research pictures from the internet or library of young girls starting from the late 1800's through the 20's, 30's, 40's, 50's all the way up to today in the 21st century. This will open up a wonderful discussion for your class and it will make this topic even more educational. Make a colorful display that will cause attention.

Discuss the way girls dress today and compare today's styles from the late 1800's to the 21st century. What changes have been made? Talk about different styles in dresses and hair. Discuss how girls talk today. Do you think they talked the same way? What do you think of girls who smoke and drink? What kind of impression does smoking and drinking give? What do they think about girls who use profanity? What does profanity say about your character?

Make a special note to tell girls not to pursue boys and explain that God has a reason why He has made boys to be 'The Pursuer.' Explain why it is so very important that they should keep their bodies pure until marriage. Explain that God will honor them with a good and happy marriage for obeying His commands. "Staying Pure Before God" is a wonderful topic you should consider using with this topic.

Being A Gentleman

You could also research pictures of young boys from the 1800's through today in the 21st century. This will be just as interesting and educational to them as well as the girls.

Read the first paragraph on page 71 with the students and have them answer them. Read all the wonderful qualities a gentleman should have. Be sure and read the last paragraph so that they will know how much fun it is for them to entertain and prepare a meal, too!!

* Follow these three exercises

Young boys respond well when you show them how they can put their manners into motion and show them how to be a true gentleman. Start with these exercises with both boys and girls:

1. *Always* opening doors and car doors for a lady.

2. Show them how to seat a lady by pulling her chair out first and then having her slip into her seat.

3. After she has finished her meal ask, "Are you finished with your meal?" If she answers, yes, then ask, "Are you ready to go?" If she says yes, go behind her chair, and as she stands up, pull it backwards so that she can comfortably slip out. Then remember to put the chair back into place.

Let every student practice these exercises twice or three times with different partners so that they can gain confidence when doing them in life.

Writing Thank You Notes

Tips and Ideas!

One of the most special ways of expressing our feelings to someone is by writing a hand written note to someone. It can also be so much fun to find the perfect card or stationery. It is especially fun to open an envelope from a friend you haven't seen in such a long time.

Mom's Tip: Prepare ahead with colorful note paper, envelopes pens, cards of the seasons, including get well, sympathy and congratulations cards for the students to choose from. *(Michael's has a wonderful inexpensive collection of cards).*

Have everyone read "How To Write Thank You Notes" and the information on page 72.

Examples of Thank You Notes: Your students will have a lot of fun writing and practicing sincere thank you notes and the proper way to write them. Help them realize how important it is to tell others how much you appreciate their thoughtfulness.

- Have the girls read the letter to Aunt Carol aloud.
- Does everyone notice Leah's sincerity?
- Did Leah tell Aunt Carol how much she liked her new cross?

How many times did she thank Aunt Carol for the cross? Why? *(because thanking her twice let's Aunt Carol know her thankful heart and your sincerity).*

Do you think it meant very much for Aunt Carol to receive a personal thank you note from Leah, or should Leah have just sent her an email or maybe do nothing at all?

(Email thank you notes <u>can never</u> replace a hand written thank you note to someone who took their time to remember you with a thoughtful gift. Always remember to write a thank you note by hand.)

Have the boys read the thank you note to Grandpa.

- Do you think Jerry was excited about his gift?
- How did he tell Grandpa was going to use it?
- How many times did he thank Grandpa for the fishing rod?
- Where were the two places Jerry thanked Grandpa?
- So, we always thank the giver of the gift at the <u>beginning</u> and at the <u>end</u> of our thank you note.

Have the students write two different sets of Thank You Notes for practice. *(You might suggest for ex. one thank you note to their parents or grand parents for giving them this special study in Christian Character and Etiquette.*

Suggestions for Writing Notes

Mom's Tip: Prepare the kinds of cards you want to use for the students to write in class. Have pens and pencils, even little stickers set at their table. The students will love to express themselves, so be sure to have colorful and interesting cards from which to choose.

Read the suggestions on page 73 of the workbook to the students. Read the work book's explanations of the kinds of thoughts to say. Have the students write special notes on each card. You might suggest them sending them in the mail, which would be a very thoughtful gesture.

Jealousy Can Eat You Up!

This is a topic children and teens need to have addressed and one they always like to discuss. The students work book on page 75 offers much information about jealousy. Read aloud to the students.

Ask where does jealousy come from? *(not from God)*

Ask the class if they have ever experienced feelings of jealousy and would they like to share their experience?

Ask if someone is having these feelings toward someone today?

Ask the students if they have noticed children or teenagers being jealous of each other. Jealousy begins at an early age.

Explain that jealousy stems from self-centeredness and insecurity. Jealousy should not be a natural way of feeling and behaving.

By feeling confident in who we are, we won't have the need to be jealous of any one, but we will want the very best for them.

Ways To End Jealousy

Page 76 offers several ways to end jealousy even before it begins. Read number 1 through 3 together with the students. This is an excellent topic for open discussion for all ages, because we experience jealousy from early childhood. Your focus in addressing jealousy is to create an awareness in each student of how precious they are to God and that He has a very special purpose for their lives. *Have all read Jeremiah 29:11.*

Jealousy Exercises

Exercises in Jealousy: Exercises 1 and 2 point how jealousy can you up with negative feelings and how wishing others the best can fill your heart with joy.

Exercises 1: Choose a boy and girl to read and portray Carla and Michael. Have them read the script first. Then have them stand and play the scene on their feet after the first reading.

Have a class discussion about Carla and Michael. Answer the work book's questions on page 77.

Exercise 2: On page 78, choose two girls to play Carrie and Allison.

- Read the script first with the class.

- Have the girls stand and portray their characters.

- Discuss the difference in the two scenes.

- Read the work book's notes about immaturity and security in who we are. Ask the students if they know where our security comes from as Christians?

Read Psalm 71:14-15 together with the students.

Be An Active Fruit: Encourage the students to practice *Kindness* this week on page 80 and to read all the reminders of how to be kind. Remind them to remember how kind Jesus was to all the people who were cruel to Him.

Weekly Lesson Review: On page 79 have the students write 5 character values they learned this week and 5 skills they can exercise to show *kindness* to everyone. Ask them to think about jealousy and if there are feelings such as this in their hearts, to go to God to help them remove them, so that they can be set free.

Closing Prayer

Week Six
Goodness

*"Learn from yesterday, live for today, hope for tomorrow.
The important thing is not to stop questioning"
Albert Einstein*

Begin The Day With Prayer

The Apostle's Pledge   *Recite with Poster*

Acts of Grace

Fruit for the Week: *Goodness*

Praise Songs

Topics: Table Manners
Manners Everywhere
Temptation Is An Opportunity
The Helmet of Salvation
What Have We Learned Together?

Fruit For Memory: *"A merry heart doeth good like Medicine"*
Proverbs 17:22

Table Manners

When you speak with your student's parents you will usually always find how much they want their children to have good manners, especially at the table. This is a special time in your students study to practice good table manners and to learn the proper ways to be a lady and a gentleman. This is also a crucial time for you to pay close attention to each student's habits and an opportunity to explain why certain habits are not acceptable at the table.

Have each student read a bullet point about manners around the table on page 83.

Mom's Tip: Please read *Creative Ideas Bring Attention Setting A Pretty Table/ Formal Dining*

This section describes what you will need for your students to experience the proper placements for their utensils, napkins, glass ware, etc. You will also find information on formal dining there as well.

First, prepare them with them with the basic rules for good table manners in their work book on page 83.

Demonstrate how to set a pretty table and invite each student to participate in your table setting exercise.

Appoint two students to be the host and hostess *(usually the oldest)*. Have them sit at either ends of the table.

It is always polite to wait until everyone is seated before starting to eat, and an aware guest waits for the hostess to begin eating. Always keep your eye on her and always use the utensils that she is using. Remind them that manners don't start and end at the table; they continue in every situation in life.

Mom's Tip: If you happen to have a combination of age groups and a few teenagers, it can be so much fun to have them work with the younger kids assisting ad helping them create a beautiful table together. *Be sure to take pictures for a keepsake!*

I Am A Quality Person
with Good Manners

In Public and On Trips

Ask several students to read the fundamental ways we can extend courtesy to every one no matter where we are on page 84.

Remind them to *always* aspire to be a "Quality Person" in every situation.

Emphasize that no matter where we might travel out of the United States, we should always be "Quality People" who always show good manners to everyone we meet.

Be sure and read the last paragraph together on page 84.

Temptation is An Opportunity
When Temptation Says Yes, I Say No

Everyone read the scripture, James 1:12 together on page 85. Discuss.

Read aloud all the paragraphs. Ask the students if they would like to share moments that they felt tempted and what did they decide to do? Did they say or did they say no?

Emphasize the Fruit of The Spirit, *Self Control,* and how we can use it to help us to be more balanced and to make right choices.

Learning to Dress in the Helmet of Salvation
Protect Your Thoughts with the Word of God

Turn to Page 86 and read Ephesians 6:13-17 and practice how to dress with spiritual covering.

How To Say No To Temptation.

Read the scene study together on page 87.

- Choose the part of Kelly.
- Choose the part of Mrs. Reid.
- Discuss and read the work book's questions.
- Read 1 Corinthians 8:16 and the questions in the work book.

These Are The Steps In Temptation's Schemes: On Page 88, read all four steps. These steps are very educational and very important for your young minds to understand.

Have them read the scripture references listed.

Discuss their meaning.

Ways That Temptation Can Be Defeated:

*Discuss the ways God helps us to resist the enemy. Read the scripture references on page 89 to hear what the devil will do if we resist him

What are three main ways we can defeat him?

1. Refocus our attention by reading God's Word.
2. Tell a friend about your struggle.
3. Pray.

* Spend a few moments and talk about memorizing scriptures and why we need them in our hearts. Ask if they can think of other reasons why memorizing scriptures are important.

Here are some examples of how God's Scriptures can be greatly helpful by:

- Witnessing to others
- Changing old habits to God's ways
- Focusing our thoughts on God and not the world
- Having a Christ like character
- Being able to resist temptation
- Understanding the will of God
- Edifying and encouraging others

Spiritual Armor

Read on page 86 all the explanations of The Helmet of Salvation

- Read The Helmet of Salvation scripture, Ephesians 6:13-17 aloud with the students.

- Explain what is the Helmet of Salvation. Why do we need it? Who is the one that protects us when we put it on? What does it do to protect us?

- Every one stand as you show them how to put on their armor before starting the day.

Begin With This Demonstration:

1. The Belt of Truth.. Put your hands around your waist.

2. The Breastplate of Righteousness.. Cross hands over chest.

3. The Gospel of Peace ..Imitate putting on your shoes.

4. The Shield of Faith...Right arm crosses to left shoulder.

5. The Helmet of Salvation... Hold both hands on either side of Your head.

Practice this exercise 2 to 3 times until it becomes familiar. Encourage the students to remember that the Helmet of Salvation is real. The Holy Spirit is with us as we put on our armor and He is faithful to protects us from harm.

Mom's Tip: For fun consider having the student's put on their "suit of armor" before leaving class. It will become a ritual they really like to do! Tell them that it is a great way to begin the day!!

Be An Active Fruit: Practice ways of showing *goodness* to others this week and include all the fruits that you have learned. See if you can be as much like Jesus as you can be.

Weekly Lesson Review: Write 5 character values you have learned this week and 5 skills you have practiced. Think about God's goodness and His goodness in you and others. What have you learned about how to say no when you are tempted? Is there a fruit that you can use that will help make you turn away and do the right thing? Is God watching you or is He too busy? Give us your thoughts. Do you believe that the Hemet of Salvation is something you need to put on every day? Why?

Close In Prayer

"God's Best Is Me"

Students Topics Review

Mom's Tip: Make an out line of all the topics you have taught during these six weeks, high lighting the most important issues for your students to retain and give a copy to each student.

Discuss each one and what the class feels about them.

Check to see how many know the meanings of the Fruits of The Spirit and how they plan to continue practicing them.

Ask if they will promise to keep the Apostle's Pledge.

Explain the importance of The Acts of Grace and that they need to always practice them and be a positive influence on others.

Ask if they feel that their appearance is important when meeting new people? Why?

What does dressing modestly mean?

Does it matter if I keep myself pure before marriage? Why?

Will God honor me with a good marriage if I promise to keep myself pure?

Does your attitude affect how you view the world?

Does your attitude affect others?

Why is being punctual important?

Ask them to tell you the definition of a Christian leader.

What does it mean to have integrity?

What is etiquette?

When did it start?

Are there different kinds of etiquette?

Who is a quality person?

Who is a non-quality person?

Who do they know is a Christian Leader?

What are the things that a Christian leader does?

Why is it important to be a Christian leader?

What do I do when I am tempted? (*there may be several other questions that may come to your mind. This is your moment to find out what they have learned and what you can go over again to make sure they have understood and comprehended the study.*)

Extra Studies
Japan and Kenya
Cultures and Etiquette

The following study of different cultures and different etiquette is a fun study of the cultures and etiquette of these two countries. Read the material first and give some thought to teaching these two cultures if you have time. It is always a BIG hit with the students, especially learning to speak a few Japanese and Kenyan phrases.

Mom's Tip: Go to "Creative Ideas Create Attention" to see what materials and games are suggested for your props and materials.

It's Fun To Learn

Different Cultures
&
Different Etiquette

Around The World

Featuring....

Japan, Asia
and
Kenya, Africa

Did you know that every country around the world has a different culture and every country around the world has different types of etiquette?

In our country did you know that we have many, many different cultures? Can you name some of them? Where did they come from? *(e.g. Italian, Irish, Mexican, East Indian, African, Russian, French, Spanish, Swedish, Scottish and many more. It is wonderful to know that almost every culture in the world is represented here in America.)*

Have you ever wondered what does **culture** mean? *It means ways we have learned and shared together as a community. These certain ways become patterns that are socially accepted and patterns we practice.* For example, in America, our families gather around the dining room table at Thanksgiving. We usually have fall decorations or a horn of plenty in the center of the table. Why do we do this? Who cooks the turkey? Who usually carves it? These are patterns or traditions our country has shared for over three centuries. We come together to celebrate how our heavenly Father, who gave us our land and who protects us, who protected the pilgrims who traveled so far across the sea, and for our forefathers who founded our wonderful land. It is a warm and close time for us to look forward to each year.

Have you ever wondered what **Etiquette** means? *First of all it is a French word pronounced like ("eh-t-ket"). It is a code we go by that is expected within a society, social class or group. Mostly, etiquette means to be <u>considerate and polite</u>.* Can you think of some ways we use proper etiquette in our society?

Let's discuss the many different kinds of etiquette we practice in America.

- Table Manners
- Telephone/Cell Phone Etiquette
- Punctuality (being on time)
- Teacher/Student Etiquette
- Conversational Skills
- Introducing Someone To Someone Else
- Proper Attire
- Writing Letters & Thank You Notes
- Respect For Authority
- Friendship Etiquette
- Good Sportsmanship
- Being Tactful (means to be considerate; thoughtful)
- Manners Everywhere
- Being A Lady/Being A Gentleman
- Opening or Holding Doors for Others
- Offering A Seat To An Older Person
- Saying "Please", Thank You", You're Welcome", and Excuse Me"

These codes of behaviors are generally practiced in other cultures, but let's take a close look at the culture and etiquette codes of the beautiful Asian country of Japan. Has anyone ever visited Japan?

Japan

(Elective Material)

Who knows where Japan is located? Japan is located in the Far East of Asia. What is Japan's capitol? Tokyo.

Japan is known for its beautiful flower gardens and the Japanese are very hospitable people who love to entertain. They are the best at preparing lovely meals for their guests. In their culture it is appropriate to offer a gift to their guest when they arrive. Usually it is a memento worth keeping. If asked to someone's home in America, we might bring flowers, or if it is a friend's birthday, a card and a gift. In Japan, their custom is the exact opposite. They give a gift to their guest to honor them.

The Japanese are very formal. They are very comfortable being quiet and still. Have you ever noticed that a Japanese person doesn't smile very much? This is a cultural pattern. It does not mean that this person is sad. When a Japanese person smiles, they can light up a room!

They are a culture with an innate sense of what is right and what is wrong. If you offer a gesture of kindness, they will offer a gesture of kindness in return. Do you think we should practice some of their patterns in America? Why?

In America we may often bring a gift to say 'thank you' for having us to a special invitation to your home *(even if the host or hostess does not expect it.)* Both patterns define our different cultures. For example, the Japanese offer slip on shoes and socks to their guests when they arrive and the guests leave their other shoes outside of the front door. Why do you think they do this?

Have you ever visited a Japanese restaurant? What do they like to eat? What kind of drink do the Japanese like to serve? Yes, hot tea! What other cultures enjoy hot tea?*(China, England)* All of these are cultural patterns that are very hospitable and distinctively Japanese.

Here Are Some Basic
Japanese Greetings:

Let's learn to say: **HELLO : Kon-nich-I-wa**
Let's learn to say: **GOODBYE: Sa-yo-na-ra**
Let's learn to say: **THANK YOU: Ari-got-toe**
Let's learn to say: **YOU'RE WELCOME: "lie lie"**

When a Japanese person hands you a business card it is with <u>both hands</u>. Isn't that interesting? It is given with a bow and is read very carefully. Is this much different from our culture? How do we hand another person our card? *We hand it with one hand and we do not bow.*

Let's ALL practice their way of giving a business card and add a bow the way they do.

A friend hands you their card and says:
   "Kon-nich ee-wa" (hello) to a new friend.

The friends says:
   "Ari-got-toe" (thank you).

Let's Take A Look At
Japanese Etiquette:

Conversation:
*Bow when greeting someone
*Do not speak loudly
*Do not blow their nose in public

*Do not display emotion
*The Japanese have difficulty saying no
*Do not put their hands in their pockets

In Business:
*Bow in greeting
*Exchange business cards
*Do not slouch

Females should avoid heels
Moments of silence are normal
Do not interrupt. Listen carefully

Dining:
*It is acceptable to make noise while eating
*Rice left in your bowl indicates the desire for seconds

*Try any foods offered
*All courses are served at once
*Cross legs at the ankle

Leisure:
*Remove shoes before Entering homes

*Wear surgical masks when they have a cold

Restaurants:
*Men sit cross-legged and women sit with their legs to the side

Culture and etiquette are two very important words, because by understanding them and practicing them, we will have a wider knowledge of why people from different countries are different from each other. Discovering other cultures and their ways of doing things makes our world so very interesting.

Let's Pretend We Are In Japan!

Jenny and Paul are on a mission trip here in Tokyo, Japan, this country's capitol. They have made friends with Su Lyn and her brother, Keioko and they have had a lot of fun together. Su Lyn and Keioko have invited Jenny and Paul over for dinner, and Paul and Jenny are real excited to see what it's like to have dinner in a Japanese home.

Who would like to portray Su Lynn and keioko?

We also need a boy and girl to portray Jenny and Paul.

(Jenny and Paul knock on the door of their new Japanese friend's door.)

Su Lynn opens the door and says: "Wataschi no ie wo kangei suru, Jenny & Paul", meaning welcome to my home in Japanese.

(She bows to them and Jenny and Paul respectfully bow in return.)

Keioko Says: "Japanese custom to take off shoes before entering house."

(Jenny and Paul take off their shoes and Su Lynn offers them sandals and socks to wear inside)

Su Lyn:
Offers their new friends from America a little gift to thank them for coming to visit them . She gestures for them to sit and relax at their table with pillows on the floor.

Keioko says:
"Come sit down and relax. Would you like a cup of hot tea?"

Jenny says: Yes. I love hot tea! It's cold outside. It will warm us up!

Su Lyn says:
"Japanese eat lots of rice." "Do Americans like rice?"

Paul says:
"Yes, we like rice, but I don't think we eat as much of it as you do!!" (they all laugh).

Su Lyn says:
"We eat rice with chop sticks. You like chop sticks?"

Jenny replied:
"Oh, yes. Chop sticks are fun!"

Let's skip forward to the end of the evening:

Jenny says:
"We had a wonderful time learning about your customs and seeing how the Japanese live, didn't we Paul?"

Paul:
"Oh, yes! I wish we had cushions to sit on at home like these *(as he fluffs them)* and I want to get some chop sticks!!"

Jenny and Paul graciously bow to them as they say Ali-gato *(meaning thank you in Japanese).*

Su Lyn and Kieoko say:
"Lie lie" *(you're welcome in Japanese)."* We had much fun having you two as our guests. You must come and visit us many times!"

Jenny and Paul say together:
"We promise to. Sa-yo-na-ra."

Su Lyn and Kieoko say together:
"Sa-yo-na-ra".

Let's pretend we are now in Kenya!

Who can tell me the location of Kenya, Africa? Kenya is located in Eastern Africa, bordering the Indian Ocean, between Jamalia and Tanzania. Who knows its capitol? <u>The capitol is Nairobi</u>. Kenya is made up 40 or more ethnic groups. Each has its own dialect. Isn't that interesting?

What are the Kenyan People like? Kenyans are friendly and hospitable people. Greetings are an important part of social and business interaction.

What Language Do The Kenyan's Speak? The Kenyan's speak English and Swahili. They also speak their own dialects which are indigenous or native to the region where they life.

Family is very important to Kenyans. They usually have a large and extended family and they treat their elderly with respect and honor.

What Do Kenyan Kids Like To Eat and Drink? They like to eat chicken, rice, goat, and tilapia. They enjoy fresh fruit and veggies. *(All good stuff!)* They like to drink tea with milk and sugar served with breakfast and at tea time in the late afternoon. Where do you think they originally got this pattern? From the British!

Kenya's Art and Artifacts: Kenya's art is known and admired around the world for its beautifully carved wood sculpture made with local materials and sold abroad. Look for museums which display Kenya's art and history. Kenya is also recognized for its hand woven baskets, jewelry, musical instruments, figurines and African sarongs.

Music and Dance: Traditional music and dance are an integral part of Kenyan social and religious lives. These two arts play an important part of Kenya culture and tradition.

Mom's Tip: Mom, since we know kids love music and are very visual by nature, you might consider going to the library and researching music from Japan and Kenya. You could also download music at home to save you a trip. Then, look on the web for interesting pictures about each culture to show the kids as you have the music playing. Show them pictures of other children and teens, nature, animals and interesting buildings. This is a fun project to do!!

*Props Preparations For Japan:

You can order on-line adorable Japanese sun hats with elastic for under the chin. Use chop sticks, bowls, tea pot, tea cups and place mats. You might even want to serve rice and tea. Create or find a low table to place all your props.

*Props Preparations For Kenya:

Find a long animal print scarf (zebra, leopard type) for the blind fold game they will soon play. African music is quite accessible to find. You might borrow some African instruments from a music education teacher at school or a music store. Go to Craigslist.com and type in musical instruments. You might find what you need there.

* **Use a Projector and Screen** or find a blank wall to show your pictures with your back ground music playing for both cultures.

* **Kenya's Most Famous Animals:** Known as "The Big 5"; lions, leopards, elephants, buffalos, and rhinos. They also have giraffes *(the world's tallest land animal)*, as well as cheetahs and zebras.

Kenya's Most Popular Sport: Kenya's most popular sport is Soccer, however their long distance runners have gained international recognition. Athletes around the world look up to Kenyan legends.

Kenyan Greetings

Let's learn to say these greetings and phrases In Kenyan Language:

Hello: *Jambo*
Goodbye: *Kwaheri*
Thank You: *Asante*
What is your name?   *Jina lako nani?*

Let's Play "Get To Know You Game"

Every one find a partner. Pretend you have never met.

No. 1 person starts by saying **Jambo** (hello) in Swahili

No .2 person also says **Jambo.** (Both smile at each other)

No. 1 person asks: **Jina lako nani?** (what is your name?)

No. 2 person answers his or her name in English.

No. 2 also asks: **Jina lako nani?**

No. 1 answers his or her name.

Let's Learn About Kenyan Etiquette:

Conversation: The hand shake is a common greeting
They engage in small talk
Kenyans do not like to say no or yes
They are humorous people
They love to laugh

Business: They use their right hand to receive gifts
They are prepared in business.
Meetings are usually long.
Kenyans prefer to make group decisions

Dining: Eating is taken very seriously
Eating is usually done in silence
Lunch is the most important meal of the day
The evening meal tends to be light
Traditional foods are eaten without utensils
using the left hand

Here is A Fun Game Kenyan Children Love To Play Called

Mbube Mbube

(Pronounced "Mboo-bay Mboo-bay)

Mom's Tip: This game uses the above scarf prop and the option to use African music.

In this game the children help the lion (mbube) to locate and capture an impala (a deer-like animal with antlers. The children begin the game standing in a circle. Two blindfolded players start the game. One player is the **Lion** and the other is the **Impala.**

- First, both the lion and impala are spun around.

- Next, the other children call out to the lion, *"mbube, mbube!!"*

- As the impala gets closer to the lion, the children shout *"mbube, mbube"* louder and louder!!!

- If the lion is far away, the children's voices get softer and softer.

- If the lion fails to catch the impala in one minute, a new lion is chosen and if the new lion catches the impala, then the games continues.

Learning about new cultures and their social behaviors and etiquette is very interesting, isn't it? Today we have learned quite a lot about two other cultures, Japan and Kenya, Africa which are located in two different areas of the world. Would you say that these two cultures are different from one another? Are they different from ours in America? In what ways do you think they may be the same? Do you think that we should practice some of the cultural patterns and etiquette of Japan and those of Kenya, Africa? Let's have a class discussion.

Creative Ideas Bring Attention

By adding a few little creative touches to your studies and work space station your children will take notice, admire your efforts and want to take a real interest in their studies. All kids are visual, so take time to prepare a colorful environment for them to see each week.

Below are some creative ideas for you to choose. Feel free to change them to fit your environment or to embellish them.

Preparing An Inviting Front Door, Study Room and Work Station For Your Children

You may only want to teach your own children, but if you plan to include other children or teens from your neighbor-hood, church or club, consider making a "Welcome To God's Best Is Me" poster or sign for the front door.

1. Choose interesting theme colors which you may want to choose for your door. For example, a red background underneath a white poster with your welcome sign is eye catching. Add red, white and blue balloons and ribbon streamers to create excitement and attention. *(these colors work well, because they are our country's patriotic colors. Or choose your own color scheme. Be creative and have fun!)*

2. Write your welcome sign on your computer using a large, legible font and print it out. Have it printed and enlarged at a print shop and place on a red poster background. Laminate. On the first day of class attach it to your front door and add your balloons, ribbons or streamers.

First Day Greeting: If you are including other new students than your children, greet each one with a warm smile and welcoming handshake and introduce yourself as their teacher. Ask each one their name and show them to their seat at their work station which should have heir own special folder for extra materials with each name on the cover.

1. Have a wide and long enough table with comfortable chairs for the number of students attending, including you.

2. To protect your table from mishaps try (*The Knowledge Tree or teacher's supply store to cover your table with colored work paper. Choose your favorite colors such as red, blue, yellow and lime green.)* Measure your table first so you will have the right amount of paper to cover your table.

3. Decorate the center of the table with a white wicker fruit basket and fill it with artificial fruit *(Michael's).* This six week study is centered around The Fruits of The Spirit which represent the character of Christ and the basket is a visual reminder of all His many wonderful attributes.

4. Buy white or different color folders for each student's extra hand-out materials. *Make sure they bring their folder with their work book and Bible every week.*

5. Write with a computer printer in large letters "God's Best Is Me" in your favorite colors and cut it out to place with double sided tape on the cover of each folder. *(use stickers to compliment your design as an option).*

6. Write each student's name in large letters on your computer. Cut out each name and tape it on the inside of the folder.

7. Place a new sharpened pencil by each folder. *(Teacher Supply stores carry colorful, encouraging pencils)*

8. Have a tray full of magic markers and high lighters for students to use.

9. Place the work book first and then the folder to the right of it.

10. You will want your students to learn Roman 12:2 which is about transformation. Spend time on this scripture, because it is so important. Our study is about transforming old habits into good and pleasing ones before the Lord. The butterfly is a good example. There are cut out butterflies that you can put on your table and butterflies that hang. *Look around and you will find them. Choose a cute hand-out, for example; a caterpillar's transformation into a beautiful butterfly.*

Your Apostle's Pledge Poster: Write the pledge out on your computer with a large enough *legible* font. Use a color back ground to draw attention. Print it and have a print shop enlarge it enough to make a poster. Laminate it to protect it. Put it on an easel and position it in your room for students to have enough space to stand and recite it easily. *Consider looking for shield- type breast plates to place over their hearts as they pledge their commitment to Jesus. (Dollar Tree may still have them.)*

The Acts of Grace Poster: Use bullet points in front of each Acts of Grace using a large, legible font. Choose another color. Print it out and have a print shop enlarge it enough to make this second poster. Laminate it. Put it on an easel next to Your Apostle's Pledge.

God's Dreams For You Posters: Find a workable space for student's to create such as a cleared away table or the floor. *(use work paper to protect your floors or carpet.)*

Materials Needed

1. Magazines: Look through your own magazines and cut out pictures about models, marriage, families, jewelry, churches, the beach, mountains, schools, colleges, cars, houses, etc.)

2. Find Colorful Posters for each student to choose.

3. 2 sets of Scissors

4. Elmer's Glue *(2 bottles)*

5. Scotch Tape

6. Glitter *(red, blue, green, gold, silver, white)*

7. Stickers *(Dollar Tree, Michaels)*

Ideas For Thank You Notes
and Writing Notes

The note paper we choose says a lot about how we think of someone. Careful attention to the appropriate choice is what we need first.

1. Choose Thank You Notes that have no writing inside. Have the student write a sincere note of thanks as explained in the students work book.

2. Select some formal and elegant thank you notes with gold or silver writing to express thanks for a formal gift or for having attended a formal occasion. *(Suggest to your students to write a formal thank you note to their parents or grand-parents thanking them for giving them the privilege to learn more about Christian character and etiquette.)*

3. For more informal thank you notes, look for ones that are colorful and ones that express a happy thought. *(Your students may choose to write an informal note instead).*

4. Make sure they address and seal their envelope and include their return address on the upper left side of their letter. Have them mail their letters.

5. Collect Birthday, Christmas, Thanksgiving, Valentines, Get Well, Congratulation and Sympathy Cards with matching envelopes. Let the students choose two different ones and have them write a special note to two different people they may have in mind.

Learning How To Set A Pretty Table

Learning to set a pretty table is always a lot of fun and educational for your students. Even six year olds can do it with a little help in the beginning. Once they learn they will likely want to volunteer to do it on a regular basis. You may want to use paper plates, cups and plastic forks, knives and spoons in the beginning so that your students can become familiar and confident setting the table without any mishaps. Add a pretty table cloth and an inexpensive flower center piece making sure it is low enough for the kids to see over. Explain why center pieces should always be low.

Materials To Set A Pretty Table

* Prepare according to the number of students you have.

* The first step is to show what is needed for the table, such as plates, cups, forks, knives, spoons, dinner glasses and napkins, salt and pepper shakers, serving trays (optional)

Show the students a picture of how a set table should look. *(Do an image search online for "table setting" and print out a picture of how a set table should look).* Show the students where to place all the utensils. Explain that formal table setting requires more than an informal table setting, which you will initially teach them using less silverware.

Demonstrate How To Set A Table

* Place the forks in order of use, to the left of the dinner plate. For example, if you will be using both a salad fork and a dinner fork, put the salad fork to the left of the dinner fork from the plate, since it will be the first used.

* Place knives to the right of the dinner plate with the rigged edge facing the dinner plate.

* Spoons are placed to the right of the knife.

* Drinking glasses are placed to the upper right of the dinner plate *(above the point of the knife)*

* The dinner napkin should be placed to the left of the dinner plate, under the forks, or placed on top of the dinner plate. *(after a meal the napkin is to be placed neatly to the left of the dinner plate, but not folded.)*

Formal Table Setting: The difference in informal and formal table setting is adding more utensils and using finer china, flatware and crystal. These are used for more formal and special occasions such as Thanks-giving or Christmas Dinner, birthdays or reception parties. Consider showing your students the following utensils used for formal dining.

* China dinner plates
* China salad plates
* China butter plates
* Crystal dinner glasses (or ice tea)
* Elegant linen or satin napkins
* Elegant napkin rings
* The dessert spoon and/or fork should be placed above
* the dinner plate
* Ice tea spoons are placed to the right of the spoon
* Appetizer forks are to be set to the *left* of the salad fork

(Choosing an informal or formal table setting is your choice. If you have students whom you feel you can trust with your fine dishes, then setting a formal table would be even be more fun.)

Mom's Tip: Be certain to emphasize how delicate china is and that it is very expensive to replace. Teach them that china is always hand washed and is never to be put into the dish washer. The same is true for silver flat wear and crystal.

Time For Table Setting Practice:

After explaining and demonstrating how to set a table, give each student an opportunity to choose each utensil and create a place setting by themselves. After each one has had a turn let them all set the table together. Clear off the table and practice it together again. Check to make sure each student has done their setting correctly.

* Choose a host and a hostess and have them sit at either ends of the table.

* Explain to the students that it is always proper to use the same utensils as the host or hostess of a home or party where you may be attending. Never begin eating before the host or hostess.

* Surprise the class with something easy you have made to have them practice using their utensils properly.

A. Consider making something easy such as a tossed green salad and warm rolls on a serving tray. Ask if they know which utensils to use? Correct them if they are wrong.

B. Choose a student to serve the class a tray of warm rolls and teach him or her to serve to each person's left. Explain that while seated, it is proper to pass food to the person to the right of you. (For example, pass a tray of chocolates offering them to the person next to you and then you may take a chocolate for yourself.)

C. Use a butter plate and butter knife for them to butter their rolls.

D. Explain that salt and pepper shakers are to be passed together. Have them all practice passing them to each other.

E. Tell the class that on graduation day they will have the privilege of serving their parents dessert while showing them what they have learned about setting the table and table manners. Mom and dad will be so proud!!

*Graduation is Fun and Satisfying for Children
and gives them a feeling of Accomplishment*

Graduation Ideas: Tell the parents and students at enrollment that you want to offer a special graduation after the completion of the six weeks study. Be sure to send out a notice when, where and what time the graduation will take place around the 4th week of class. Ask for an RSVP and how many friends and relatives will be attending.

Tell your students to give you a count.

Preparing For Graduation:

1. Find excellent attendance or participation certificates at an office supply store. Write each student's name, the date and sign your name as teacher.

2. Order brass medallions with red white and blue ribbons. (engrave **"I'm God's Very Best"** and the student's name on their medallions. You can find engraving at a trophy shop or service online.

3. Make a **Fruit of The Spirit Double Layered Cake** (easy)

   1 lemon cake mix
   1 strawberry cake mix

2 cream cheese icing toppings in cans using your favorite
fruits in a large Pyrex dish
*add ice cream if desired

Follow directions on cake packages. Cool each cake and remove from cake pans. Ice one layer and place the other layer on top. Ice both cakes on top and on the sides. Add your fresh fruit and decorate to your liking. *(this cake is delicious, easy and a big hit with the kids, because they love all the Fruits of The Spirit. Serves 20 to 25.)*

* Students seat and serve their parents and grandparents the Fruit of The Spirit Cake at the end of graduation. *(practice seating and serving 2 weeks before graduation.)*

Option:

4. Make a Fruit of The Spirit Salad (optional).

   i.   Large fruit bowl
   ii. Butter lettuce placed in bottom of bowl
   iii. Lots of fresh fruit
   iv. Poppy Seed dressing (mix together)
   v.   Lime Sherbet and Ginger Ale Punch

5. Punch:

    a. Glass punch bowl
    b. Lime sherbet (2 half gal.)
    c. Ginger Ale (2 liters)
    d. Cool Whip (lg. tub
    e. I pkg. frozen strawberries thawed

* Mix all together. It will look very frothy and inviting. This is a delicious, easy punch to prepare for all ages.

* Decorate the sides of the punch bowl with oranges, grapes and pineapples.

All these preparations are easy and so much fun to put together for your students. You are making memories to last for years to come and even a life time.

6. Serve the Fruit of the Spirit Cake or Fruit of the Spirit Salad on china salad plate.

7. Find elegant napkins to match the china.

8. Use salad forks

Don't forget your camera!

Dear MOM,

Please let me take a few moments to express how happy I am that you have taken this step to teach your own children Christian etiquette and character yourself, instead of relying on other secular programs or teachers! As mentioned in the beginning, no one knows or has more influence upon your children better than you.

I hope so much that you have truly enjoyed every moment shared with your children and hopefully other students teaching **"God's Best Is Me."** I also hope that this **"God's Best is Your Child"** Teacher's Guide has been helpful to you. How could anything be more rewarding than seeing your children become more and more like Christ as they spend quality time studying His character, and etiquette? What could be more satisfying than to know you are the one who taught them? I am so proud of you!

This study began in the early 90's when I was asked to teach music for an after school program in Memphis, Tennessee. I had no idea that one day I would be sharing my experiences and all these topics with you, encouraging you to take the ball and run with it your way. I pray in my heart that you have been personally enriched by teaching and touching your children's lives, as well as others. It is also my prayer that if it is God's will, you will feel the passion that I do to continue "on and on" reaching and teaching other children in your neighborhood, schools clubs churches and organizations. When you do you will be doing something major in this world, not just to educate our children and youth, but you will be doing it by imparting the most value lessons in their Christian walk as they learn and imitate the character, etiquette and leadership of Jesus.

In Christ's Work,
Dr. Jeanne

Please feel free to contact me at:
JeanneSheffieldThD@gmail.com
www.SouthernGracePlaceUSA.com
202-716-6444

God's Best Is Your Child
Marketing Plan

Teaching Children & Teens
Character & Etiquette

Now that you have experienced teaching your own children this six week course, consider the possibility of *reaching out* and making a real difference touching many other young lives teaching Christian character and etiquette, and at the same time earning an excellent income.

As a home school teacher of a Christian character and etiquette study, you can not only enrich the lives of Christian children, but you can reach many secular environments that do not embrace Christian beliefs. The challenge will be easy to adapt some of the topics from this study appropriately and creativity. You will find that many people and organizations will respond to you positively and you will have more opportunity to reach many more children with the character and etiquette of Christ than you had thought possible.

On the following pages are several marketing and promotional ideas for turning these lessons into a positive and potentially profitable business.

Ideas For Marketing This Course

* Ebooks: There are many on-line resources on how to market a business. Search engines will point you to numerous web sites on this topic. Other specific ideas are detailed below.

Reach Out To Home School Mothers: Find lists of home school moms and personally call them about your classes. Ask them the ages of their children and send them a flyer announcing your registration and information about your classes starting soon. Inquire if you could send them extra flyers to share with other home school moms.

Reach Out To Teachers: with children ages 6 to 8, 9 to 12, 13 to 17 in both Christian and secular schools and academies.

Visit Principals: of elementary, middle and high schools both public and private with materials and pictures to leave with them. Explain your business. *(Always call and make an appointment to meet prospective principals, head masters and teachers in person).*

Give A PTA Meeting Presentation: use creative visuals of two or three topics that would be interesting and appropriate for your parents and teachers. Include your audience to portray scene studies with you. Make it interactive! Have flyers to give to everyone at the meeting. Be personable and excited about your new classes coming up and leave them with a positive impression.

Give a Home School Meeting Presentation Choose a couple of topics that mothers may want their children to learn, and present highlights of some topics in the "God's Best Is Me" Student Work Book. *(Answer any questions.)* Always bring a sign up sheet and pens with you everywhere you go.

Contact Your Pastor/ Youth Pastor: Inquire if he would consider giving you space to teach your classes. Ask if he would give you a few moments during the Sunday morning or Wednesday night service to announce your classes and tell a little bit about them. Approach the youth pastor if you could teach a topic one Sunday to his class and bring your work book's CD for them to sing a couple of fun praise songs.

Contact Community Centers/ YMCAS: See if your local community center or YMCA would be willing if they would schedule a 6 week slot for you to teach classes there. Bring a card Table *(use an attractive cover for it)* and display a sign up sheet, registration dates, times and location of your classes. Leave a tri-fold poster display with your name and telephone number in large letters and numbers for parents to contact you.

Offer Summer Camps: Schedule a week or two week summer camp character & etiquette class at a community center, church or retreat.

Give A Community Library Presentation: Choose 2 or 3 topics and include students to participate

Contact Librarians of Grammar Schools, Middle

Schools and High Schools: Librarians are always looking for interesting presentations and you have the best! Give a flyer to all the librarians to post and to all the students announcing your new registration for your upcoming classes. Ask them to give the flyer to parents.

Make A Professional Packet Presentation: Include pictures of students with an attractive logo on your business card that catches attention. Always leave your card with prospective parents, teachers, pastors, and leaders of organizations. Don't forget friends. Let everyone see your enthusiasm and love for teaching their children. Explain briefly how and why these studies will make a great difference in their lives.

You Are Your Very First Presentation: Set an example by

looking the part of a well dressed and immaculately groomed teacher of Christian character and etiquette. Every time you give a presentation or meet a prospective parent, client and teach a class, it causes everyone to take notice and want to be a part of your studies by having a sharp, well-groomed appearance.

Get Your Logo Working: Visit Vista Prints on line for reasonable promotion material. Your logo works for you on your business cards, business stationery, invoices, receipts, business publications, and your advertising.

Optional! Take out a newspaper ad, or promote your business on the side of your vehicle. It's a plus to add your logo on all your promotional materials you hand-out or sell, such as t-shirts, mugs, calendars, pens and pencils.

Ask For Referrals: Don't be shy in asking parents or teachers to refer your studies with other parents. Give them promotional materials as you write them and even at graduation. You'll be sure to get a positive response.

Etiquette Presentation Parties: Ask moms to host etiquette parties in their homes. *(Offer a discount on their child's tuition)*

Invite moms and daughters over to an afternoon tea. Create a theme. Use china tea cups, saucers and offer cookies, tea or lemonade. Give a presentation including moms and daughters. Play "God's Best Is Me" CD to familiarize the moms and daughters with the music your students will sing in class.

Play Games: *(See "Creative Ideas Create Attention")*

Have A Drawing: Offer a surprise gift. Put numbers under chairs. Draw a number. *(This is a perfect setting for you to introduce your studies and to announce when your classes will begin. Be prepared to have your registration papers and all materials on display for them to see.)*

Have A Pizza Get Together: Invite boys and girls over for an afternoon pizza get together with moms and dads. Offer lemonade and root beer. Play a few games with their parents and listen to the CD. This will be a real hit with everyone, especially the kids and you will be off and running with your foot in the door to teaching all the kids there! *(Remember to be prepared!!!)*

Ask For Mom Volunteers: Ask them to distribute and post flyers for you. *(Moms are always willing to help when they believe in you).*

Video Tape Your Classes: If you are already busy teaching classes, video tape some of your on-going classes and have it looped so that it continually plays when you rent a booth to market your business. You could also have it play when new prospective parents come into your home or business space.

Create An Eye-Catching Display Table: Place student's pictures and captions underneath. Talk with moms who walk by and give them a new flyer. Ask them to sign up their child for your next class or to sign a call back sheet with their name and telephone number.

Create Your Very Own Web Site: Check out CraigsList. com for web site designers or look around for other designer sites; there are plenty of them out there. Explain your ideas and give them your budget. Ask to see examples of their work and price.

Having your own web site makes you more professional and gives you credibility and freedom to post schedules, dates and newsletter info. It is also a great way for parents to view all that your studies offer. It saves you time and money from having to send flyers and other materials by mail. You also have the option of linking your site with other complimentary sites.

Become A Blogger: Post important comments about your Business. Write favorable quotes parents, students, teachers and organizations say about your studies.

Get Networked Online: The Internet is a great way to market your own online business. A Google search will turn up lots of topics related to leadership and etiquette. Sign up for a no-cost account with one that relates with what you do and set up your profile. (some examples of personal networking sites are facebook. com, twitter.com, biznik.com, and LinkedIn.com)

Say Thanks: Write a thank you note to anyone who has helped you along the way. Everyone appreciates being valued.

Start Pod Casting: It is a great opportunity to speak and be heard by adding your audio to your blog or your web site. The easiest way to do this is to contact a nifty little free service at: http://www.utterli.com that lets you record your pod casts by phone. Simple!

Offer Your Expertise: Write some articles about your experiences teaching. Give advice for those things that have worked and those that haven't. Biznik is a terrific place to do this, and there are plenty more options out there. Find one targeted to your area and have fun!

Print Post Card Mailers: Print a clear, concise, "want to see it again" ad on a small, colorful post card and mail it to prospective parents, teachers, and organizations. *People like smaller cards to keep for reminders.*

Advertise: Glance through ads in magazines and notice that a great ad concentrates on solving a problem. You are in the problem solving business of correcting old habits and replacing low integrity with God's integrity and developing strong Christian character. Write catchy, interesting ads about the benefits of a child or teenager studying your program. Use testimonials from students, parents, teachers, etc.

Get Free publicity: The more times your business is mentioned in the newspaper, the better. Publicity brings you more students. Call local columnists, editors, reporters who are always looking for stories. Don't be shy. You have to blow your own horn, but use finesse.

Create An Event: Invite local editors and reporters to attend. Place a free ad in the local event section or workshop section of your newspaper. Give the newspaper plenty of time to post your event.

Pair Up with Other Similar Organizations: This is your opportunity to spread the word about your work and to develop repertoire and support with others trying to make a positive difference in the world like you. Partners who cross-promote have a big marketing pay off, because partners can successfully expand through each other's customer's base. Be on the look out for a good, ethical partner.

Give A Free Seminar: This is a wonderful way to draw new parents ad students causing interest from the newspapers to write a featured article on your business.

Cable TV Advertising: Companies offer ideas for small business budgets from advertising on their TV guide listings or through running infomercials.

Radio Advertising: Radio is still a viable way to reach moms driving to and from school who listen to Christian radio. In time, when your budget allows, you might consider blocking out a series of radio spots before school starts up again or during the holidays. Offer your listeners a special rate for the first 25 callers or a gift certificate. You may even consider writing and producing your own spots. If you have expressive kids, include them in your spot. Radio is expensive but a lot of fun!

E Mail Advertising: Develop an email advertising list, so you can communicate with current parents. Be clear in your "Subject:" line exactly who you are and what you represent to avoid mistaking your email for spam.

Dear Mom,

This is an exciting, rewarding venture. It is something you will love with all of your heart like I do knowing the difference you are making in young lives. Please feel free to call and ask me any questions or offer new ideas that you have found teaching or marketing your own Christian character & etiquette business. You and I and so many other moms are partners in this wonderful endeavor together reaching out and touching young lives all over America in our churches, schools, community centers, clubs and organizations. This is God's work coming through us pouring over and into the hearts and minds of our kids and teens. We are imparting the most important, valuable and foundational Christian education our children will ever need to build a future based on the solid principles, character and impeccable etiquette of Christ.

As author and teacher of "God's Best Is Me" and author of your teacher's guide, "God's Best Is Your Child", I want to be here to encourage you in every way I can and to support all your efforts getting started and during the process. You are <u>not</u> alone. You will have a monthly newsletter to give you ideas and an opportunity to share your experiences with what works, what doesn't. To read my monthly newsletter go to:

www.SouthernGracePlaceUSA.com

Look for the newsletter link, "God's Best Is Your Child" Newsletter.

Thanks again for choosing this study not only for your child, but for giving yourself the joy of reaching out further to our children and teens and spreading your own wings. The sky's the limit to all those young children and teens whose hearts and minds will be blessed to have you bring out God's very best in them. God bless you and every single child who walks into your class.

Bringing Out The Best In Kids Together,
Dr. Jeanne

God Brings Out The Very Best In Me

Words &Music By Jeanne Sheffield

I'm learning how to love
Learning how to share
I'm learning how to give
Learning more to care

Opening my heart
Offering my hand
To my fellow man

I'm watching what I say
I'm watching what I do
Making sure I pray
Not just for me, but you

And every single day
In every single way
I can see the change in me
God brings out the very best in me
Yes, God brings out the very best in me

Every day in every way
God brings out the best in me

Repeat Song
Offering my hand
To help my fellow man

I Walk in Grace

Words & Music by Jeanne Sheffield

I walk in grace
I walk in love
I walk in grace
Sent from heaven above

I walk in grace
I walk in love
I walk in grace
God's loving grace

And I am growing stronger
I am growing tall
Following the footsteps
Of the great Apostle Paul

I walk in grace
I walk with Christ
I walk in grace
I am proud He's my life

And I am growing stronger
I am growing tall
Following the footsteps
Of the great Apostle Paul

Walking in grace
Walking in grace
Here I am a child of God
Walking in grace

The Fruit of the Spirit

Author Unknown
(VBS song to the tune of "If You're Happy and You Know It)

Oh the fruit of the spirit's not an apple
Oh the fruit of the spirit's not an apple
If you want to be an apple
Then you might as well hear it
You can't be a fruit of the spirit
'Cause they are Love, Joy, Peace, Patience, Kindness, Goodness,
Faithfulness, Gentleness, and Self-Control!

Oh the fruit of the spirit's not a grape
Oh the fruit of the spirit's not a grape
If you want to be a grape
Then you might as well hear it
You can't be a fruit of the spirit
'Cause they are Love, Joy, Peace, Patience, Kindness, Goodness,
Faithfulness, Gentleness, and Self-Control!

Oh the fruit of the spirit's not a lemon
Oh the fruit of the spirit's not a lemon
If you want to be a lemon
Then you might as well hear it
You can't be a fruit of the spirit
'Cause they are Love, Joy, Peace, Patience, Kindness, Goodness,
Faithfulness, Gentleness, and Self-Control!

Oh the fruit of the spirit's not a banana
Oh the fruit of the spirit's not a banana
If you want to be a banana
Then you might as well hear it
You can't be a fruit of the spirit
'Cause they are Love, Joy, Peace, Patience, Kindness, Goodness,
Faithfulness, Gentleness, and Self-Control!

Love Stretches My Heart

Words & Music by Jeanne Sheffield

Love stretches my heart
And makes me big inside!

Love stretches my heart
And makes me big inside!

God's love stretches
God's love stretches
God's love stretches
When you open your heart wide (end here)
Repeat:

And I am God's own vessel
Overflowing with His love
Yes, I am God's own vessel
These two arms were made to hug

Yes I am God's vessel
My purpose here is clear
I'll show the world that Jesus lives
He lives inside of here

Back to top:

Attitude Says A Lot

Words & Music by Jeanne Sheffield

Verse 1
Attitude, Attitude
Is how you wake up and greet the day, hey!

Verse 2
Attitude, Attitude
Shows up in every little word you say!

Chorus
Attitude can be positive (speak)
It can be quite negative, too
Attitude is a choice you make (sing)
It all depends on you! (speak)

Verse 3
Attitude, Attitude
Makes people wanna stop and notice you!
(who me? Yes!)

Repeat Chorus

Verse 5
Attitude, Attitude
Says you're happy with the way you are!

Verse 6
Attitude, Attitude
Says you can wish on a falling star! Ah....(sigh)!

Repeat Chorus

End
Attitude is in your gratitude
So let's be thankful to God each day (yeah!)
Attitude says a lot! (speak)

Always Be Kind, Always Be Gentle

Words & Music by Jeanne Sheffield

Always be kind
Always be gentle
Give from your heart
Show that you care

Always be kind
When somebody needs you
Be a good friend
Loyal and true

Chorus:
Your smile
Is all it takes
To wash away a tear
Your hug can mean so much
When someone's
Lost their way

Always be kind
Always be gentle
Put someone first
Before yourself

Always be kind
And understanding
God is watching you
Making sure that you
Are following His commandments

So, always be kind
And gentle to everyone

A Real Good Friend

Words & Music by Jeanne Sheffield

Are you a real good friend?
Can I count on you?
Are you a real good friend?
Loyal, honest and true?

Chorus:
'Cause if you
I have found a treasure
yeah, if you are
I'm the lucky one

'Cause if you are
We;ll be close friends forever
Sharin' the good times
Carein' through the hard times
Lovin' life because
We've found a friend

Are you a real good friend?
One to tell my secrets to?
Are you a real good friend?
Make me smile when I'm blue?

Repeat Chorus:

End: I think I've found a real good friend

Sweet Joy

Words & Music by Jeanne Sheffield

I've got joy overflowing
I've got joy down to my soul
I've got joy and it's growing
Gonna get me more and more

I've got joy in the mornin'
When I meet the risin' sun
So much joy keeps on growin'
For my Father and His Son

Sweet Joy
Sweet Joy
Nothin' can compete
With this happiness so sweet

Sweet Joy
Sweet Joy
Livin' in the presence of sweet joy

I've got joy overflowin'
Blessin' every one I meet
Joy keeps pourin' down from heaven
And it's absolutely free

Sweet Joy
Sweet Joy
Nothin' can compare
To the joy you'll want to share

Sweet Joy
Sweet Joy
Livin' in the presence of sweet joy
Livin' in the presence of sweet joy

Peace, Be Still

Words & Music by Jeanne Sheffield

Sometimes when you're worried
Sometimes when you're scared
Sometimes when you're frightened
And nobody's there

Sometimes when you're lonely
Sometimes when you cry
Sometimes when you lose
The dearest person in your life

Give it up to Jesus
He'll calm you in the storm
Give it up to Jesus
He'll keep you safe and warm

Peace, Be still
Peace, Be still

Sometimes when you're hurried
Sometimes when you fall
Sometimes when you live alone
And there's no one you can call

Sometimes when your heart breaks
Sometimes when love ends
Sometimes when your future
Is lookin' mighty dim

Give it up to Jesus
He'll calm you in the storm
Give it up to Jesus
He'll keep you safe and warm
Peace, Be still, Peace, Be still

Be a Package of Goodness

Words & Music by Jeanne Sheffield

Be a package of goodness
To everyone you know
Be a package of goodness
No matter where you go

Be a package of goodness
Wrap yourself in one big bow
And soon you'll find
Your love will overflow

Overflow, Overflow
Overflow, Overflow
Be a package of goodness
And let your love overflow

Be a package of goodness
Show 'em a great big smile
Be a package of goodness
Come on, let's go the extra mile

Be a package of goodness
To everyone you meet
And soon you'll find your love will overflow
Overflow, Overflow
Overflow, Overflow

Be a package of goodness
A package of goodness
A package of goodness

And soon you'll find your love will Overflow

The Circle of Love

Words & Music by Jeanne Sheffield and Celia McRee

The circle of love is an endless connection
A chain of affection for all
The circle of love is a world full of laughter
Where nobody cries if they fall, even if they're small

The circle of love has no start and no finish
And everyone in it is a friend
The circle of love doesn't have any limit
So why don't you come right on in
To the circle of love, the circle of love, the circle of love

The circle of love is like finding a rainbow
Where all of your dreams do come true
The circle of love is like playing in sunshine
Where blue skies are always in view, Shining down on you

The circle of love is like being a princess
A knight dressed in armor, a king
Anything you can dream
So come on and let's sing (la, la's…)

The circle of love has its arms all around you
Love around you're in the middle of joy
The circle of love is so happy it found you
Everyone, be it girl, be it boy
Doesn't matter, it's great to be here
Here in the circle of love (Repeat la la's…)

The circle of love keeps on going forever
And doesn't care whether you're tall or small
Young or old, king or queen
You can be anything

Be all your dreams
Be in the circle of love (repeat)

Come Take My Hand

Words & Music by Jeanne Sheffield

Come take my hand
Let's go down by the river
Come take my hand and let's meet the Lord
I understand He loves all of His children
He loves to sing and He laughs when we play

Come take my hand
Let's go down by the river
We'll be surprised at the children we see
All of them loving His glorious presence
Wanting a kiss on the cheek

Come and go down to the river with me
We'll meet the Master who sets the world free!

Come take my hand
Children of God
Let's all join hands
Let's praise the Lord (Repeat)

Let's go and meet Him (solo)
I heard he tells stories
Filling our hearts with such wonderful Joy!
Don't be surprised if He already knows us (solo)
He watches over whenever we sleep

Come and go down to the river with me
We'll meet the Master who sets the world free!
Let's all join hands
Children of God
Let's go and praise the Lord
Come take my hand
What a new exciting experience
This will be!

Patient Spirit

Words & Music by Jeanne Sheffield

Please God, give me Your patience
When I want things to go my way

Please God, give me Your patience
Help me to live like you everyday

Chorus:
And help me to be gentle
Kind and considerate
Being calm and so together
Give me your patient spirit

Please God, give me Your spirit
Show me what you would do

Please God, give me Your spirit
I always want to please You

Chorus:
And help me to be gentle
Kind and considerate
Being calm and so together
Give me your patient spirit

To start my day
To start my day
Hear me when I pray